Stealing the Show

9 points to help you get your

organization noticed

Richard Bliss

rbliss@blisscorp.com
www.blisspoint.us
Printed by: Lulu Press, Inc.
3101 Hillsborough Street
Raleigh, NC 27607

Contents

C820

As we grow up, our experiences allow us to write a unique life story. Each story defines who we are and who we have become. The stories I'm going to share were the result of my experiences growing up, mostly as a result of my "nomadic childhood." I realized as a young businessman that those experiences helped to shape my perception of the world, especially when it came to my profession.

Here's what I'm talking about: I started Kindergarten in Pullman, Washington while my parents attended Washington State University. Our family circumstances changed, and my mother, brother and I moved to Spokane, WA, where I attended 1st grade at Cooper Elementary School. So far, this might sound similar to your childhood. But my family's circumstances changed yet again and I was suddenly attending another school in the first grade *for a month.*

During my 2nd grade year, we moved again, I was attending another school, and it's one that I remember because I got lost the first day on my way home. 3rd grade was spent in three different schools: two in Fairbanks, Alaska and the other somewhere in Idaho. 4th grade meant moving back to Spokane and attending Blake Elementary.

I attended the 5th Grade at Wells Elementary in Wells, Minnesota.

Then in 6th grade, something happened that had never happened before: I started school at the same place where I had finished the year before! Sadly, this new experience lasted only a month or so. After starting the 6th grade at Wells Elementary, we moved back to Spokane, where I attended a school with a name that I just cannot remember. Towards the end of my 6th grade year, we moved to Tekoa, Washington and I attended Tekoa Elementary.

A few months later we moved back to Spokane where I attended Blake Elementary (again). This was cool because I remember this kid coming up to me and saying he remembered me from the 4th grade. After only a month of attendance at Blake Elementary we moved again. This time, I got to attend Holmes Elementary, which as I recall was a tall, multi-storied brick building surrounded by asphalt and tall chain-link fences. On April 26, 1975, my family moved again and I finished my 6th grade year at Chinook Elementary in Lacey, WA.

From September of 1974 to May of 1975 I attended six different schools as a sixth grader. In total, during the seven years of my elementary education, I had attended 14 schools in four different states. And because I had been thrust into new environments without any friends or familiar faces over and over again, it helped to shape me in many ways.

First, I had to develop survival skills and I applied a certain cleverness that allowed me to function in each new setting, with its unique rules, customs, and traditions.

Seldom do we realize how much of our life experience is built on collective assumptions. Here's what I mean by that: "common sense" only works when a common group of people collectively agree on a common set of standards. My "nomadic childhood" experiences taught me that each city, each school, each classroom, each group of students

2

had its own set of common sense standards that made sense to them. Those standards are often times not the same from group to group or city to city.

As I moved in and out and amongst these diverse groups of students, I learned to read the mood of a room and I learned that the smile is rather powerful when it comes to breaking down barriers. I learned to identify with others and to empathize and sometimes sense their emotions. Because my perspective was always that of someone on the outside looking in, I learned to stop and connect my ideas and then see things from that different perspective.

I learned how it felt to be alone and to be excluded from the "In" crowd. I also learned how to build my own crowd, based on inclusion and mutual respect. Above all else I learned to not be afraid to try anything, and to never let fear get in the way of living my life the way I wanted to live it. And the results have been pretty amazing thus far.

This book is a collection of stories that relate what I'd like to call "BlissPoints." A BlissPoint is an essential nugget of truth – My truth. But these truths are things that I've learned and experienced. Truths that have given me a different way of looking at a situation, of going against traditional thinking, of seeing things that others have missed and most importantly, they are truths that have yielded success. They are examples of how I well...stole the show, and moved the spotlight away from the traditional and focused it on the unusual or the unique. Each point relates a situation where I was able to achieve success by looking at things as I did as a youth: from a different perspective.

BlissPoint #1: The Art of the Giveaway

When you move with your family as much as I did as a little boy, you develop an interesting relationship with material things. Sometimes you have to decide at a young age which things you value and which things aren't as important. When we moved, I would only get to take a few toys with me. There were times when my brother and I only had a moment's notice to gather our belongings, and say goodbye to Scruffy, before we were shuffled into the car and on our way. With that practice having been repeated over and over, it now means that there aren't any toys that survived my childhood, and there are only a few photos that remain. Well, it's those few things and one special item that have made it this far. By some miracle, I still have my trumpet that I've had since the 5th grade. My mother knew that my father had played and she thought I should play too. To this day, my 5 children are amazed when I pull the trumpet out from under the bed, warm it up, and begin to play a few notes from the songs I remember. If you can place value on only one thing you'd better recognize its worth and you'd better make it count.

Have you ever attended a tradeshow and stayed until the end of the event, when the vendors attempt to give away all their leftover stuff? The yellow duckies, the orange hats, coozies, the mouse pads, pens, t-shirts...leftover stuff to anyone who will take it.

If you have, then you have probably also seen the "professional tradeshow junkies." They are the people walking around carrying bags stuffed with every single free thing they could get their hands on. Let's be honest: tradeshow giveaways are one of the reasons why some people attend. Think of all of the thought, the effort, the time, and the money that went into making that free stuff available in the right color with the proper logo placement. But where does all of that free stuff go when it gets home? It becomes what I like to refer to as a "landfill item." Almost as soon as it gets there, it either goes into the bottom of the toy box, Spot is chewing on it, or it goes right into the garbage can.

I have been to countless tradeshows over the years and am still dismayed at the completely unoriginal ideas that I see. These stress squishy thingies are most often the repeat offender. How many of them do we really need in the world? Believe it or not, your stress squishy does little to build your brand or generate sales leads of any kind.

Here's something else to consider: when you hear someone say, "Can I get another one of these? I have two kids," you know you have missed your target. Toys and trinkets are not good giveaways. They appear to be at first glance, because someone with children might be drawn to your booth and may want to give you their information in order to solve their problem of what free souvenir they can grab. But ultimately, this cheapens your brand, diluting it to a worthless kid's toy.

So what makes a good giveaway and keeps your well-thought-out free items from ending up in a landfill?

Here are three questions to ask:

1. Would it sit on someone's desk or be used on a daily basis?
2. What kind of value does this item have?
3. Is it something worthwhile that I'd like to have?

Make it Original

Oftentimes one of the main challenges with any kind of cool giveaway is the cost. When considering cost, there are three types of giveaways:

- The spiffy "Boy, I can use this" or "mass-giveaway" or "Landfill" type
- The bigger than life, grand-prize drawing type
- The "stop-by-our-booth," or "jump-through-a-hoop," and we give you something type

You already know what I mean by the last one, so let's talk about the spiffy kind of giveaway first. And don't hesitate to be controversial. One of the most spiffy *and* memorable giveaways I was involved with was a packaged condom branded with my corporate logo (By the way, this was also a great example of believing in my team).

Kyle and Dean, my marketing managers, came to me with an idea for our next event. They wanted to give away condoms and I'll get to the reason why in a bit. I understood what they wanted to do and the direct connection to our messaging. It was going to be risky and this idea didn't go over easily, but, I strongly believe in letting your team experiment and appropriately defending them for taking risks. I also wanted to let their idea have a chance at success.

The more it was discussed, the more I was able to discern that the condoms were going to be the cool thing to give away. Then again, no one—except for us three—was willing to be associated with it.

The giveaway condoms became a kind of secret giveaway. Why? Once they found out our idea, the show owners wouldn't allow me to give them away openly in my booth. I wanted to have a bowl for people to help themselves. You see, I was an email anti-virus vendor during the time that the "I Love You," "Melissa," and other devastating email viruses were crippling systems around the world. The condoms would become personal anti-virus protection or "Software for your Hardware," and I had about 500 of them to give away. Without permission to openly display them, I had to be more creative, and what I did instead was a lot more fun and a lot more memorable.

I kept about 25 of them in my pocket at all times. As a friend or acquaintance would come up, I would pull one out and show them the cool thing I was giving away and then lamented about how terrible it was that because of the rules, I couldn't openly give the condoms away. But! I was I willing to gift it to them, as long as they kept it quiet.

Of course—and as I suspected—nobody was able to keep quiet once they got one, and pretty soon my booth became a "distribution" site. People who I didn't know would approach me. They would look around cautiously and say something like, "I'm supposed to ask about some kind of giveaway that you have." I would look around cautiously, pretending to make sure no one was looking, then reach into my pocket and hand them one or two. Sometimes, my cautious looks would catch the eyes other people nearby who would also witness the exchange. After person A would leave, person B who had witnessed what happened would approach me and would inquire about what had gone down. I would reach into my pocket and repeat my story.

It didn't take long before word had spread to a large portion of the conference attendees that they needed to stop by my booth. I had no trouble distributing the 500 packets I had, while sharing a bit about my product, and I

7

had done it with very little noise but a tremendous amount of attention.

Although a number of years have since passed, to this day, I'm approached by people who still remember and oftentimes still have their "personal protection." My response: You know that those things have an expiration date, right?

Make it. Don't buy it.

Oftentimes we get trapped in a rut, only able to deliver what is placed before us. With the advent of globalization, a whole new world of opportunity has opened before us. Now, if you see something cool you want to give away, you can create it yourself. It has become much easier to actually produce your own cool giveaway, rather than to buy someone else's.

My best example for this is the GWAVA Mouse: a USB mouse with a transparent portion that is filled with green water and clear oil. The corporate logo floats in the liquid. The water and oil don't mix, so a layer of green is overlaid with a clear layer of oil. The logo floats on one layer and sinks in the other, causing it to appear to float in the middle. And when it's used, the mouse glows in green—our corporate color.

This giveaway would normally be prohibitively expensive, ranging from $20 to $30 each. With global markets just a mouse-click away, you can design your own cool products and have them made rather inexpensively. My team contacted a manufacturer in China, told them what we wanted, sent over a prototype, and when the design was approved, we ordered several thousand at $4 each.

At that price, I could afford to give every attendee one of our custom-designed mice. It is the most popular booth giveaway I have ever done. Everyone wanted one, and you know that they took them to their office to parade the cool thing that they had received at the show. My mission was accomplished. The weeklong event was remembered mostly by the very cool and worthwhile giveaway that I put into the hands of nearly every attendee.

Make it Memorable

The opposite extreme to giving away the "spiffies" is the big giveaway. This can do as much to generate attention as the cool items you are handing out to everyone, and you don't have to go to extremes on this effort to make an impact.

I sponsored a golf event along with several other vendors. There were about 200 people attending and as vendors, we were allowed to put something in the giveaway bag. Suggestions from the event coordinators included golf towels, golf tees, golf divot repair tools, and a list of other rather uninspiring golf-related items.

The total cost of our giveaway items, at this low number, was going to run between $300 and $500. Instead, I thought to focus on the emotional appeal. These people liked to golf and I wanted to generate a more memorable experience.

I contacted PING, a sports-equipment manufacturer, explained that I was sponsoring a golfing event and that I wanted to feature their golf equipment as a giveaway. I asked if they would be willing to sell me an entire set of clubs, with drivers, a putter, and bag.

They agreed to discount a full set, retail price $1,500, for $800! So I dipped a little deeper into the budget.

I brought the bag and clubs to the event and told the event coordinators what I had as a giveaway. Originally, I had signed up for the smallest sponsorship, a single hole. However, once they saw what I was willing to deliver as a prize, my sponsorship was automatically upgraded to an official event co-sponsor, and I was given the chance to speak before the entire group at dinner and to present the prize. This would have never happened if I had bought some branded golf towels.

This giveaway worked so well, the following year we did it again and this time everyone was looking forward to winning my set of clubs. The winner from the previous year was there as a judge, and wanted to win again since his wife had confiscated his new set of clubs the moment he got home.

Make it Count

If you are going to put forth the effort to place something in the hands of your prospects, remember that they will judge your product, your service, and your company by the quality of the gift and the emotional impact it makes on their lives. Be sure to give them something they'll remember...something worthwhile. Make it count.

BlissPoint #2: Heart vs. Head

Because I grew up on the move, I missed out on a lot of what was happening around me. The Vietnam War, the Space Race, the Cold War, sports events, and just about anything else that would require you to have to pay attention and listen to world events, blew right past me. My memories of that time are simply a blank when it comes to events outside of my own personal drama. I do have one memory that has stayed with me. It starts in a farmhouse kitchen, early on a winter morning with the sky still dark as night and the winter cold threatening on the other side of the door.

I am seated there at the table eating chocolate oatmeal for breakfast and listening to the radio. We listened to the same program every morning. I remember the feeling that the show created for me. It was one of amazement, surprise, and of a blossoming hunger to know more. I can even sing the jingle from the Northwest Orient Airlines commercial, but the part that has stayed with me all these years, was the ending of the radio program. It ended the same way every morning, and for those of you who are old enough to remember, you know what it means when I say, "And now you know the REST of the story." Thank you Paul Harvey. You gave me those wonderful memories. I don't remember what you said in your stories, but I know how you made me feel.

"They may forget what you said, but they will never forget how you made them feel." - Carl W. Buechner

When I am about to speak in public, this is the quote that I repeat to myself, right before I walk on stage. I remind myself that the words that I say don't matter as much as the emotion that I give to those words. That's what people listen for. Carl Buechner said it so well.

Think back to the last time you listened to someone who inspired you. Think about the person who you love to hear speak and could listen to over and over again. For some, this person may be a charismatic speaker like Billy Graham, or the Great Communicator, Ronald Reagan. Bill Clinton was also able to use his speaking capabilities as a way to influence people.

There is a secret ingredient at work here amongst these individuals. They understand the power in the emotion of their words over the power of the words themselves. Believe it or not, but this doesn't happen through the things we say. It also happens with the things that we write. A press release, a marketing brochure, or a blog entry can carry an emotional impact beyond the written words themselves.

Here is an example. One year, a major vendor and my biggest partner canceled their annual technology conference in Salt Lake City, Utah. As one of the biggest sponsors of the conference, I received a phone call hours before the announcement went public.

Although there were less than 3 months before the event would take place, many attendees had already purchased airline tickets and made hotel reservations. Hotel reservations can be canceled—airline tickets cannot, without paying a penalty.

Understanding this issue, I immediately generated several press releases. The first was an announcement of my own conference and that people could attend mine instead. I knew they had the budget already allocated. The challenge was that my conference was in 3 weeks, not three months, and people needed time to get approval for travel.

As I noted the comments from customers on the forums, it became clear that a major challenge to their attendance was the cost of the change fees. You see, our event was in Las Vegas and not in Salt Lake City.

I generated a second press release that was aimed at the emotional audience rather than the literal audience. My announcement was this: my company would pay ALL change fees for any person needing to change their flight from SLC to LAS in order to attend my conference.

The CFO flipped! He began ranting about the costs of making this kind of announcement. Nothing against CFOs, my mother and brother both fall under this category and I love them to death, but on occasion they can be a little too literal.

Don't get me wrong. It is human behavior to moan and complain when your expectations are quickly dashed and naturally, you become emotionally upset. But this kind of situation required that the response become focused on the emotional need rather than the literal issue. By announcing that I would pay for the fees, the general public suddenly felt that there was a company who understood their condition and was willing to help.

Oftentimes, by simply having someone recognize the pain, the condition, or the issue, it will be enough to pacify the angriest customer. We received a tremendous amount of goodwill from our gesture.

People were simply astounded that a company would be willing to do something like that. But that is the key: we were willing, even though the cost was uncertain.

Human behavior also says that a kind gesture is often met with a kind gesture in return. In this case, even though we were willing, no one actually came forward to take us up on the offer. We had a record attendance for our conference that year, and although many people had to change their flights, no one went through the effort to have us reimburse them even though we were willing to do so.

Addressing the emotional need of the customer and taking a perceived risk to assist or provide a solution will always win over addressing the literal need and playing it safe.

The e-Grinch

At the dawn of the Internet age almost all email traffic was carried across 14.4 modems. Remember those? And remember how quickly your email was received when it came across an upgraded 56k blazing speedy modem?

During this time my team and I created a new kind of service: the hosted model for providing email management services. Today it is called The Cloud, but back then no one really understood what that meant.

The idea was to reroute email to my servers, scan it for viruses, porn, or spam, and then send the clean items back onto the Internet and off to the customer's email server.

The challenge back then wasn't necessarily the spam or porn, but it was attachments themselves. Because everyone used dial-up connections for their corporate email, if someone attached a big file it would slow down the entire server bringing everyone's email to a halt. And back then a big file was about 1 MB.

Here was the challenge: I had to convince people that there was a problem, invisible to the end user and misunderstood by the executive. Email was so new, people didn't think twice about sending anything to everyone.

So I launched a PR campaign to communicate my service to an audience that didn't understand my solution because they didn't understand the problem.

It was the Fall and people were beginning to attach these cute Christmas card files to each other. These were the executable files that when opened, would show flying reindeer, or dancing elves, and there was one particular file that showed snowmen having sex—not something you really wanted being passed around the office.

However, there wasn't any way to stop it and once someone received the first one, they would want to "share the joy" with their friends and co-workers. So as people hit the forward button, unbeknownst to them, they would easily flood their company's fragile email system with Holiday wishes.

My service was designed to block viruses but I immediately realized that it could block EXE files just as easily. Therefore, I had two choices for a press release headline.

New service prevents executable files from being distributed by electronic messaging systems.

or

Free blocking of all Christmas Card files between now and New Year's Day.

I sent out a press release with the second headline. Any corporation in the world could sign up for a free service. It was late October and my service already offered a 30 day free trial, this simply extended it an additional 30 days. In addition, my service could do a lot more than simply block Christmas card files, but that wasn't the point. I was going for the emotional impact of the problem that IT Administrators were screaming to CEOs:

"STOP LETTING PEOPLE SEND DANCING ELVES! IT IS CRASHING THE SERVERS!"

Like a holiday miracle, the timing was perfect. I was suddenly a hot story, with trade magazines giving our little company a tremendous amount of coverage.

Then we hit the big time. The story found its way to the desk of Marsha Walton, Science and Technology Editor for CNN. I received a call from Marsha that she would like to bring a camera crew to our offices and film a story about this new crisis that we were battling.

CNN came and did their story and ran it several times on Headline News. As the story ran, CNN came up with a catchy name: the e-Grinch. My service was ruining all the opportunities for people to send holiday cheer to their neighbors, but to IT Admins, I was Santa Claus, bringing them some nice holiday cheer and no crashing email servers.

BlissPoint #3: Break the Barriers

I know what it is like to feel alone in a room full of people. As a kid, I had to walk into a new school and a new classroom every year where I didn't know a single person. And I had to do it over and over again. All of the repeated instances brought me to a decision early on: unless I wanted to continue to be all by myself, the responsibility was on my shoulders to fix the situation. And I did. The new 3rd grade kid walked into the classroom and he immediately spotted a very cute girl. Her name was Star. She was quiet and shy and I really wanted to meet her. We were about to play a game called "Heads Up, Seven Up." This was my chance! The teacher picked seven kids, who went to the front of the class. The teacher would say, 'Heads down, thumbs up!" Everyone else put their heads down and their thumbs up.

The seven of us would meander through the rows of desks and each of us would pick one person, by touching their thumb. If your thumb was touched, you hid it. Then the seven of us would return to the front of the class, and the teacher would say, "Heads up, seven up!" Everyone would raise their heads, and the seven whose thumbs had been touched would stand up and guess which of us had touched their thumb. When I was one of the seven, I picked Star every single time. After the fourth time she finally figured out it was me. I had found a way to break the ice and get her to notice me. I was thrilled....and then we moved.

What did your mother always tell you? Don't talk to strangers. As children, this is beneficial wisdom. But unfortunately, this advice has carried over to our business world today. It is nearly impossible to get anyone to talk to someone they don't know. The mindset of not talking to strangers makes it nearly impossible for businesses or business people in a casual setting to mix and mingle. People just don't like talking to strangers.

To address this issue, you must discover new ways of interacting with your audience. The question is this: how do you make a social business reception with vendors and customers into a memorable experience that brings value?

Having fun and making things into a bit of a game is always a great way to break down barriers. However, you know that listening to a vendor make a product pitch can be anything but fun. Alternatively, being a vendor and attempting to force people to make eye contact with you so you can attempt to sell them something is not a pleasant experience. Many times, companies will not send their highly skilled salespeople or even the more social people to these events. Instead, they send techies— people who really are not interested in the buying or the selling aspect of the business transaction but are more interested in the "how it works" side of the business.

Speed Dating, Techie Style

During an early part of my career, I hosted a reception. The room was filled with music from a live band, the lights were turned down low, a large amount of alcohol and finger foods were being consumed, and there was a lot of talk and laughter. The thing that struck me was how the room had become segregated.

The vendors, in front of their little pop-up stands, circled the room conversing with each other, while the guests huddled in the center of the room like wildebeests avoiding the lions.

The vendors weren't talking to the attendees and the attendees weren't talking to the vendors.

I went back to my office after the event and thought about how to fix this problem which was this: how to overcome the inherent shyness that people naturally have when talking to someone they don't know and the fear that they have about becoming trapped by the overanxious vendor or attendee.

Speed Dating, techie style, was born.

I have to admit...the first time I presented the idea to my team, I was met with silence. No one was quite sure what I was talking about. At that point, even though they didn't say it, I knew they were pretty sure it wouldn't work. The good news was that I had the trust of my team and had their willingness to give it a try. I was the boss, and that didn't hurt, either. Besides, if it failed, there was only going to be one person who got the finger-pointing: me.

The next step was explaining it to my vendors and sponsors. Again, the idea of "Speed Dating – Techie Style" was met with silence and a bit of confusion. However, they also trusted that something good would come of it and they were willing to go along.

Here's how it worked.

The evening started off with a dinner sponsored by the vendors. This ensured almost everyone at the conference was in attendance. Free food is hard to pass up.

On arrival and before they sat down to the meal, each attendee received a random number from one to 15, and a stamp card. Each of the 15 vendors was assigned a number. At the end of dinner, the each person was instructed to match the number they received to the vendor's booth number and go to the specific booth.

With 300 attendees and 15 vendors, this put 20 people in front of each vendor's booth.

When time started, each vendor was given 90 seconds to pitch their product or service to the small, yet captive crowd. It was all simultaneous. When I said "Go!" the room erupted like a carnival midway! Each vendor began shouting out their 90-second pitch.

When time was up, each crowd member received a stamp on their card acknowledging they had listened to the pitch. Then, each crowd moved to the adjacent vendor's booth on the right.

It took about 90 seconds for the groups to move, and then with time announced, the vendors did it all over again, shouting out their 90-second pitch.

With a total of three minutes for pitch and move, it took about 45 minutes for everyone to circle the room and listen to each vendor give their pitch. The stamp cards were collected, everyone sat back down, and free products were given away.

The vendors loved the experience! In 45 minutes they were able to make their pitch to nearly 100% of the attendees. I say nearly 100% because there was an open bar during the event and some attendees kept running back and forth to the bar in between the pitches.

In addition to the presentation opportunity, the vendors also admitted that being given only 90 seconds forced them to distill their message to the main points. They had to focus on what was most important to their audience and then address that problem or solution as quickly and succinctly as possible.

Several of the vendors switched presenters, which allowed multiple members of their staff the chance to practice making the product pitch. But, according to the vendors, the best part of the Speed Dating event was the steady amount of post-event traffic that held up for the rest of the show, as interested attendees returned to get more details or ask questions.

And the attendees? They loved the experience. In less than an hour, they were able to hear each vendors pitch. Many of the attendees admitted that they would not have approached the vendors on their own, and now they had found new solutions they were looking for.

BlissPoint Speed Dating has been successfully deployed for several years. Vendors continue to share with me that there is no other single event that they have ever done, that has been as successful at finding new leads and new business opportunities as my Speed Dating idea for these kinds of events.

How's that for talking to strangers?

BlissPoint #4: The Bug Hunt

Before the Internet and console video games we all shared a common bond with card games and board games. When making a new friend in a new town and a new school, board games were often the bond that gave us a common ground to get to know each other. My grandmother taught me to play Pinochle, my Grandfather taught me Cribbage, my mother played Life, Stratego, Monopoly, Clue, Careers, and many others. Games were easy to share and quick to play. I developed a life-long love for the joy and the thrill of playing games. Even today, my oldest friends are those who also share this joy: Michael P., Jeff M., Scott L., John R., and my brothers Rodney and John. Great friends make great memories.

As a vendor, there is no better place to stand out in a crowd than a trade show. If you have done your homework properly, then the show has a tight group of pre-qualified contacts. All of those people are there for a similar reason: they are looking to buy what you are looking to sell.

If you have ever been to an industry trade show, you recognize one thing: they are incredibly boring. Okay, so not all shows are boring, but the vast majority of trade show floors are a large collection of vendors, desperate to talk to anyone who will make eye contact with them. That means that we, as attendees, walk through the trade show by staring at the tops of the booths or looking at peoples shoes. We never look anyone in the eye.

There is nothing worse than being a vendor at a show and being ignored. It just isn't little vendors, either. Big vendors have the same problem of trying to figure out how to pull people into their booth.

As a vendor you have to find a way to break through this communication barrier. You have to change the game, literally.

Let me introduce you to The Bug Hunt—a traffic builder. Attendees receive those little cards they carry around to a group of vendors, they get a stamp, and then return the cards for a chance to win a prize.

Occasionally, the trade show coordinator will have a traffic builder that you can participate in for a fee. What I have discovered over the years is that oftentimes, the show vendors don't even think about doing a traffic builder, and if they do, it is usually something incredibly lame.

The key to a successful traffic builder is generating excitement and gaining collective buy-in. If your trade show coordinator isn't doing a traffic builder, then you should be doing one yourself.

Let me say that again in another way.

You should never exhibit at a trade show without participating in or sponsoring a traffic builder, even if you have to create one yourself.

For example, my company was a small vendor at a big show. Our product was a bit geeky and techie and we were competing with a lot of other vendors for the limited attention of the attendees.

I decided to do my first traffic builder. Because there was a pirate theme for the vendor night with the attendees, I ran with that. I contacted a dozen other vendors who were exhibiting at the show. Just called them up and made a pitch.

If they agreed, they got to participate in my traffic builder in exchange for a nominal fee, which would go towards the prizes. The grand prize was airfare for two and a hotel stay in the Caribbean. Cost was about $1,500. There were three second place prizes: a personal DVD player and a copy of movie *Pirates of the Caribbean*. The cost was about $1,000. With the remaining vendor participation fee and some of my own budget money, I gave away 10 - 3rd place prizes. Each prize was a bag of $100 in gold Sacajawea dollar coins. 10 x $100 = $1,000 for the 3rd prize.

In all, the prizes cost about $3,500. I created a pirate treasure map with all of the sponsors and their logos and booth numbers creatively placed on the map. The map was given to all attendees in their conference bag or as they passed our booth during the week. (Just so you know, the map's placement inside the conference bag was a bust since most people throw everything away that is inside and just use the bag.)

When the participants presented their map at the specific vendor booth, they got a stamp of confirmation. They filled out the completed map and turned it in at our booth. The requirement was that the participants be present to win. So we dressed up in our best pirate outfits, and gave stuff away at the designated hour. There was a large crowd at the booth—much bigger than we had planned (This was a good problem to have, but since the crowd size made it difficult to hear, it meant that we had to plan better the following year).

Each year, as we attended the same show, the Bug Hunt traffic builder got bigger and bigger. At one point we had to get a double-decker booth to stand on because the crowd size had swelled into the thousands.

Picture this: You're at someone else's show, and you have thousands of attendees at your booth, chanting your company name. You're throwing t-shirts into the crowds and are giving away so much stuff that it takes nearly 45 minutes for you to give it all away. I've done it and you can do it too.

Any show can become yours by putting together your own traffic builder.

Here are some pointers to remember:

Get at least three other vendors to participate, even if you have to give away the sponsorship the first year. By having multiple vendors involved it creates a sense of energy and inclusion. People like to be part of something, and multiple vendors helps to create a sense of importance to the traffic builder.

Give something away for participation. We gave away cool things to those who would go through the process. Most years it was one of the cool mice that I'd mentioned before...the one with the floating bug. Some years it was a Skype headset, and another year it was a laser pen and pointer. Whatever it is, make it cool so that the item alone is worth their effort.

Make the prizes worth something. If you are going through the effort to give a prize away make it worth something. Don't give away the same game console that everyone else has at their booth. Instead, be creative. One year, when *Lord of the Rings* on Blu-ray had just come out, we gave away reproductions as prizes. One winner walked away with the Sword of Aragorn, another with the Staff of Gandalf, and the last with the Helm of Elendil. In addition, a lucky winner got to take home a 50" Plasma with Blu-ray player and the movie. If you make it an emotional prize, the attendees will go crazy for it.

Be bold and go for it! If a vendor isn't sure about participating, then sign them up anyway, and ask for the money *after* the event. If you aren't sure whether a traffic builder is allowed, check to make sure, but don't let it stop you if you can't find out.

We had a show that we went to each year and each year the *"DO NOT DO THIS"* book produced by the event host, got thicker and thicker. Why? Each year they would include a number of restrictions to the activities that we had done the year before. If you are first you can get away with it once. Always be first!

BlissPoint #5: Narrowing Your Focus

Every school has them and we all experienced them in some way or another. So...which clique did you belong to when you were in school? Can you remember? I played the violin, the trumpet, and the tuba in the band. I wrote science-fiction stories and poetry. I was in drama, on the basketball team, the football team, was a male cheerleader, played with computers, and was nicknamed "the Kissing Bandit." I won a blue ribbon for my pig at the County Fair, was a member of 4H, played Ice Hockey, and went fishing and camping in Circle, Alaska. These activities were all a part of my childhood before I finished the 6th grade.

I wasn't all of these things at the same time. But each time I entered a new place I became a new person to those who saw me for the first time. Each time I arrived in the school, I had to decide how I was going to be identified. What I was going to be known for? I couldn't be all of these things at the same time. What I could do was focus on who I wanted to be without having to be everything to everybody. Because when you try to be everything to everybody you become no body. And just so you know, the Kissing Bandit first made his appearance in Kindergarten...at the ripe old age of 5.

Hummers in Las Vegas

Here is the challenge: you have a very limited budget and are exhibiting at the largest tradeshow in the United States—an event with more than 125,000 people in attendance. How do you stand out and get noticed?

My first year in attendance at Comdex in Las Vegas, we spent $10,000 on a small booth that was located on the backside of someone else's booth on the backside of one of the outer show halls. I think 6 people wandered by my booth in the week that I was standing there.

Not a great return on investment. The next year we stole the show on the same $10,000.

The following year, rather than targeting the random people who may walk by our booth, we instead focused on influencing the influencers. More than 1,000 press credentials were issued for this show. If there was a way for us to get in front of this audience, they would have the power to get in front of a much bigger audience, an audience much larger than the 125,000 people in attendance.

The idea was to target every member of the press and business analyst by focusing on two things they value: their money and their time.

In Las Vegas, at a major show like this with such large number of people attending, the cab lines can be horrendous. You often wait up to two hours to simply catch a cab. Our idea was simple. We would make ourselves available to the press as a free shuttle service. Unbeknownst to them, this would be a shuttle service they would never forget.

We targeted the press with a special pre-show mailer which was a simple post card with the picture of one of the new Hummers on the front. This was at a time when the they had just hit the market, and the new models were the updated military-style versions, but they still rode on those immense tires. On the back of the card was a brief message with my cell phone number. It was mailed to all of the press contacts. The message said this:

Get taken for a ride! Don't stand in the cab lines at the show. Call me and I will have a Hummer pick you up and take you anywhere you want to go in Las Vegas for free. The only catch? You get to listen to a pitch about why my company is the best.

Next, we flew to Huntington Beach and rented five of the vehicles. We put our logo and web address on the sides of the vehicles and drove them to Las Vegas in a convoy. The vehicles were so wide and intimidating, that the only vehicle that didn't get out of our way was a cement truck. We pulled into town and made a very big impression, even by Las Vegas standards.

Next, we got a suite in a hotel, set up a dispatch center with a bank of radios, and my cell phone. My administrative assistant staffed the center.

Approximately 700 members of the press and business analysts called my cell phone number that week and they all were taken for a ride. They called in the morning to be taken to breakfast meetings, called in the afternoon to be taken to lunch meetings, and called in the evening to be taken to dinner. Others called at the beginning of the show to be picked up from the airport and called at the end of the show to be returned to the airport. 700 people and 700 interviews.

It was a spectacular success.

My company was written about, talked about, and commented about all over the world, from Chile to Sweden, Australia to Austria. We became the hit of the show and stole the attention with the tiny budget that funded the big idea. I remember I got coverage in the Miami Herald because the Technology reporter had gone to Las Vegas but had not received my post card, so they never got a ride. This was great! People who I had never even met were writing about me.

We didn't attempt to talk to everyone at Comdex. We simply focused on a single group of people and made them the target. And the success went far beyond the amount of money we spent.

Influence the Influencers

During the great surge of mobility devices in 2003, when Smartphones were just hitting the market, we attended a show of about 5,000 people. We were just breaking into the market and needed a way to stand out without spending lot of money to do so. By working with several vendors, a major carrier, and several smartphone vendors, our plan was to target key individuals: the executives, the planners, channel partners, and members of the largest users group. Each of these individuals received a free smartphone and 2 months of free service.

With a giveaway of 150 free Smartphones and with those selectively placed devices, we were able to get name recognition, product recognition, and exposure that went far beyond a drawing or prize giveaway. Because we had spread the costs between the carrier and device manufacturer, there wasn't a single large burden for one vendor to carry.

This is a major point: whenever you attempt to do anything with marketing, always find a way to align your interests with those of the other vendors, so that you can maximize your efforts while minimizing your costs.

Posted: NO SURFING

During the dawn of the Internet age for businesses in 1995, although companies began to scramble to get on the Internet, not everyone was thrilled with the idea.

At the time I had been working with a large number of law firms by helping them upgrade their systems to Windows and to begin moving to the Internet. When you work with a law firm, it's all about billable hours. And after the software upgrades, some of the lawyers had noticed that Windows computers seemed to make their employees less productive. It didn't help that Microsoft shipped Solitaire with every Windows machine.

With employees having access to the Internet, a lot of law practices saw the opportunity for distraction increase dramatically with the new idea of "web surfing."

I know this sounds crazy for those of you who grew up with the Web being everywhere, but trust me, for a time, companies legitimately worried that their productivity would plummet because their employees would be spending all their time on the Internet.

As I watched the news, I noticed something interesting about the way people talked about the Internet. To them, email and web surfing were seen as the same thing, they were simply "The Internet." But as an email expert, I knew differently. I worked with companies every day, helping them set up their email systems to be able to exchange email across the Internet, and that task didn't have anything to do with websites and web pages.

I also discovered that most people didn't understand that their email system or server could connect to the Internet without their web browser having to connect. This point was a revelation to me, so I wrote a letter to the editor of a weekly national computer magazine to explain the difference between email connectivity and web connectivity. To my great surprise, they published my letter.

As I continued my work at the Law firms and while talking to the lawyers and partners, it became clear that these companies wanted to be on the Internet, but didn't really know what was required. You see, when my clients spoke to IT Admins, the techie's idea of "The Internet" included a full-blown Internet connection—something which was so expensive (approximately 60k per year, for web surfing alone) that it drove away customers.

But when my clients would be out playing golf or chatting business over drinks, one of their new acquaintances would hand them a classy business card that had theirname@theircompany.com, noted under their name and business phone numbers.

To my clients, to the lawyers, and to the other business people who had this same desire, they all had this collective assumption, and this is what they meant when they said they wanted "to be on the Internet." They wanted to have their own domain name and to have their own email address. They didn't care about websites. It was all about the email connection

At the time, my company was launching an innovative solution that allowed a company to connect their current email system to the Internet for about $99 a month...a solution that could be easily accomplished without the $60k internet connection price tag.

It was innovative and unique! But being innovative and unique can be a bad thing when you are attempting to get noticed. If you have something so new that people can't easily categorize it and it's so new that people aren't familiar with what it does by comparing it to something they do know, then it becomes rather difficult to get your message to stick in their minds.

We had the solution, but no one was listening. We just couldn't get our message across. We were getting desperate. If we didn't figure out a way to get customers soon we would have to shut down the business.

We turned to advertising to find a way to tell our story and met with our ad agency. They presented one idea after another about how our service worked. There was a lot of discussion back and forth about presenting a good image that conveyed our value proposition. However, no one could agree on what the value proposition really was.

None of the ideas seemed to capture the uniqueness of what we were doing. I thought back on my letter to the editor, and I realized that what we really needed to convey, was this: what people thought about email and the Internet was wrong.

We needed to run a 'negative' ad targeted at the worry and cost that represented the collective thinking of what the Internet was all about. I wanted to tell people that surfing the Internet, one of the biggest fears for connecting to the Internet, could be solved by using our service.

My idea went over like a lead balloon. The thought of the 'negative ad' was definitely *not* met by a unanimous decision of agreement in my favor. The ad agency didn't like having to define something we were not. The technical management of my company wanted to tell more about the gee-whiz way we had solved a technical problem. To the credit of the ad agency, they took my ideas, and came back with a mock-up.

The ad consisted of a wooded sign stuck in the sand that said:

POSTED: No Surfing

The tagline?

How to connect your entire company's email system to the Internet without giving them all a day at the beach.

Sold! We went for it.

At the time there were nearly a dozen corporate email products in use in the world. We put the logo of nearly every one of them on the ad. We then placed "$99 a month" in a big circle in the corner, and other product information on the ad as well.

There was so much information, that the ad team admitted that they had never created such a "busy" ad before. It was too much information in their opinion. My reasoning behind the abundance of information was that I did not have enough resources to help people make a buying decision. The ad had to convince them all by itself.

Once the ad was done we decided to run it as a full page on the inside front cover of the magazine that had printed my letter to the editor. We had spent ALL of our marketing money. Not just all of the money for the year, but literally all of our money. If this didn't work, we would all be looking for new jobs.

The ad was run on a Monday morning. We arrived to work, and I was there especially early because I was nervous. It was do or die time, sink or swim, soar like an eagle, or crash and burn.

I watched the clock as it approached 9 A.M., Eastern Time. We turned on the phones. You can imagine my surprise when they immediately began to ring. We didn't have any sales people. It was just me! So I began taking the calls. When the receptionist arrived, she began taking calls as well, and then the other admins, and the support staff, and then anyone who wasn't doing something absolutely critical, they were on the phones, too.

The phones kept ringing and ringing and ringing. We took 200 calls the first day, 300 on the second day and nearly 400 the following day. At nearly 1,000 calls, we weren't even through the first week.

The ad had struck a nerve. It had communicated something very specific that people were very concerned about, and they responded! One caller, a technical person asking for more information, stated that their non-technical boss had come running into the room, slapped our ad down on the desk and said, "Call this company right now! This is *exactly* what we need!"

Stories like these kept coming in. Even some of my previous law office clients had seen the light and contacted us. The service we were offering was the perfect product at the perfect time, but without the perfect message, we wouldn't have gone anywhere.

The success of this campaign was that we focused on a very narrow message with a very narrow solution. We didn't try to do everything for everyone. We did one thing and we did it very well, and we found a way to communicate it succinctly.

The company was successful enough with this campaign that they grew revenue, and were acquired for $55 million, and no, I didn't get any.

To be successful, know your audience and tell a focused story.

BlissPoint #6: Go ahead. Grab the Microphone!

I have a memory of sitting in the very back of my grade school classroom. I'm in the last row, furthest from the door. The school was an ancient brick building with wooden floors, tall windows, and a massive chalkboard in the front. We were doing multiplication tables and each row was in competition with the other rows. The teacher asked for one student to come forward to represent their row to compete. No one's hand went up except for mine. I didn't know anyone, and I didn't have any fear of failure. There weren't any expectations that I was pressured to live up to. Instead, I simply wanted to stand out and show my skills. And if I sat on my hands, I would never be noticed.

The teacher picked me to come forward to the towering blackboard, along with five other students, one from each row. There was a tall list of multiplication equations. On her signal we were to finish the problems as quickly as we could and then go back to our seat. When she said "Go," I began flying through the equations, not even worrying about the classroom watching from behind. Instead, in a very short time, I finished my list and quickly returned to my seat. After sitting down I realized that the other kids were hardly halfway through their columns. They kept worrying about the kids sitting behind them, and were constantly turning around, with looks of embarrassment. Some of them never finished the work. You've got skills, right? Seek out chances to show them! If you don't, no one will know about them, and you may not get another opportunity.

Taking Chances and Stepping Out

Sometimes you just have to stick your neck out and push when you know you are right about your ideas.

When I was a young 1st Lieutenant Artillery officer I had attended some of my training in Wyoming. It's easy to shoot big guns in Wyoming, when there's not much chance of hitting anything. During the two weeks that we were in the field, General Dennis Reimer, US Army Forces Commander visited the training base. He was a four-star General and would later become Chief of Staff for the Army.

Needless to say, it was a big deal that he was coming to visit our Battalion. During the planning meeting, it was determined that General Reimer would only have enough time to visit one unit, or Battery, within the Battalion. Amazingly, my unit was selected. As the Executive Officer, I was responsible for the operation of the six guns in the Battery. But I was a junior officer, very junior compared to a four-star general, but I felt that our unit needed to do something memorable. We needed to stand out and ensure that this visit was well remembered by our soldiers and by the Commanding General himself.

I had an idea, but it was met with hesitation by my Captain and the Battalion Commander. They didn't want to do anything too far out of the ordinary. I urged them to allow me to handle the arrival plans and I promised that it would not embarrass my commanding officers. I was successful in my persuasion and was allowed to put on my show.

Here was my plan: We were already out in the middle of the desert for training. The artillery guns were lined up in a zigzag line, in the form of a "W," with about 50 to 100 yards between each gun. Each gun was manned by five to

10 man crews. General Reimer was going to flying in by helicopter, and land at one end of the gun line, and then walk the gun line, while meeting each gun section in turn.

The morning of his visit, we practiced our routine with all the soldiers. When the helicopter came into view, I stood behind the center of my gun line and called all the men to attention. Each gun section lined up in a straight line behind their gun. Then, as the helicopter passed low overhead, I had the entire Battery come to Present Arms, with all of the men saluting the helicopter as it flew by.

We held the salute until the helicopter landed, the General exited and my commanding officer returned his salute to the General. There was about 150-200 yards distance from where the "guideon" and I were standing and everyone else. I imagine that it must have been an unusual site for us to be standing so far away, *and* saluting the air, with nearly 100 men lined up behind me doing the same thing.

As soon as the General returned the salute of my commanding officer, I shouted, "Order Arms!" This was the order for the men to drop their hands to their sides and remain standing at attention. Because of the long distances between the gun sections involved and because of the noise from the helicopter, it was impossible for my voice to be heard. But I had thought of that too. I had a battle flag positioned next to me. The men watched the flag and followed the orders based on what they saw the flag do, rather than listening for my orders.

Once we dropped our salute, I had all six gun sections race back to their guns and fire a one round salute to the General. This was six guns going off, firing artillery rounds down range.

Then, as the General began moving up the gun line, each gun would reload their gun, wait for the General to enter, then once he entered their area, they would fire off their gun again in salute.

The plan went off without a hitch. The General moved down the gun line with each gun going off in order as he approached. At the end of the inspection and visit, just as the General was heading back to his helicopter, he turned to my commanding officer and said, "I wanted to let you know that I saw all your men at attention from my helicopter as I flew over and I very much appreciated it. Thank you."

This was a case where my unit, my soldiers, and my commanding officers were able to receive a compliment and thank you for one of the highest ranking officers in the US Military. It didn't matter who got the credit, what mattered is that we took a risk at standing out by making the situation about our guest, and he noticed it and appreciated it.

When given the opportunity to do something beyond the norm, don't hesitate to step out and take a chance. You will be surprised at the results. Go on, be a star!

Making the Most of Press Releases

When it comes to press releases, here is something I tell my team on a regular basis:

Only 3 people read your press release: you, your competitor, and your mother.

No one else really cares and almost no one takes the time to read the whole thing. However, with that said, press releases do serve an important role in marketing and you need to learn how to write them properly.

First, let's talk about why you're writing a press release in the first place.

It is supposed to announce news or to communicate an important piece of information that people should know. It's about something that is significant and relevant. It is not supposed to tell the reader everything about your product or service.

Many press releases tend to be written by well-meaning marketing people. The documents are written like a marketing brochure, explaining all of the features and all of the benefits of their wonderful product or service. Again, this is not the purpose of the press release. Although it is a piece of marketing literature, it does not serve the same function as a marketing brochure. It's design is simply this: convey news.

In addition—and this might surprise you—the audience of your press release is not your customers. It is written for editors and writers. The people who you are attempting to influence to write more about your product or service.

Here are my six BlissPoints to writing a great press release.

#1 The Headline - Create an Emotional Appeal
The headline is the most important element of a press release. It's that big bold statement at the top that says it all, saying, "Here is why you should care."

It contains the elements of what the release is about and what the real news is. It should be a single line if possible and each word is capitalized.

For some, this seems to be the hardest part of writing the release. Do your best to create that emotional punch. The headline should make the person want to read what follows, without a doubt.

WARNING.

In today's environment, where press releases are picked up on the Internet and listed by news organizations, it is important to read your press release headline in fragments. Here's an example of a mistake I made on a press release for a major release of our product.

Our solution provided Disaster Recovery for a different company's email product: GroupWise.

Here was the headline for the press release:

GWAVA Releases Version 3.1 of Its Novell GroupWise Disaster Recovery Product.

Unfortunately for me, and regrettably for Novell, the Internet posted the heading like this:

GWAVA Releases Version 3.1 of Its Novell GroupWise Disaster...

The product release intended to be a positive and was quickly turned into a negative because of how I put the words together and how the Internet truncated my sentence. I learned my lesson and now am careful about how a headline appears in a shortened version.

In addition, because of the truncating issue, it is important to put the key words at the beginning of your headline so that they appear when listed in search engine results.

As far as the emotion, a press release is like shouting to the world. If you are going to shout something, be sure to make it sound exciting, interesting, and compelling.

#2 Important Stuff Goes First

Press releases must tell a story. They must draw a reader in from the moment they begin reading. Moreover, remember, the reader in this case, is the editor who is looking for a story to write about something that interests them, because they usually share the interests and likes of their audience. Impress the editor and they will think it will impress their readers.

The headline is the first thing they read. Make it the most important.

The first paragraph must contain nearly all the important information so that if the reader stopped after the first paragraph, they would have learned everything they needed to know to form an opinion about the release.

3 Keep it Short and Simple

The rest of the body of the press release should fit on a single page. Nobody likes to read press releases and the editors will not read it either—they will scan it. They will not extend that scan to a second page. Your contact information and boilerplate company information can appear on the second page, but the body should always stay on the first page.

You are attempting to compete with hundreds of other press releases that the editors and content managers are wading through. You aren't going to get noticed or written about if you force someone to read what you have to say.

#4 Quotes

Quotes can certainly help a press release. It causes the reader to stop and look at who said what and consider why they should care. If you have a recognizable name included in your quote, it immediately communicates a tremendous amount of information to an editor. Your credibility and importance go up by five points.

However, with that said, it isn't mandatory that you have a quote. I have had some companies refuse to run a press release because a quote couldn't be found in time to make the deadline. Quotes help, but don't build your press release around the quote.

While we are on the topic of quotes, here is a way to increase your chances of getting a quote. Don't email the contact and ask them to send you a quote to put into your press release, marketing brochure, or web site.

Instead, write up a quote that is complimentary but not overly gushing and send it to the person you want to quote and ask them whether the quote you have written is okay to publish. Oftentimes they will get back to you with a modification. Make it as easy as possible for the person you want to quote.

Just remember, when you are reading a quote from anyone, there is a really really good chance that person never actually said that, they simply signed off on someone else saying it for them.

#5 Audience: Remember...Three people!

Okay, maybe I'm exaggerating when I say that only three people will read your press release. Nevertheless, you must remember that a press release is intended to be an extremely focused piece of marketing material. It should speak as closely to the editor or audience as possible, by telling a story that is very specific to the interests of the readers themselves.

When it comes to appeasing an editor, a great way to find out what they are interested in is to read the articles they have written, the topics they cover, and the items that have generated the most comments. By knowing the interests of the audience, that will get you noticed.

#6 Stick to the Purpose

A press release was originally created to allow a company to communicate with media editors in a quick and efficient manner, whether that editor worked for a television station, a national or local newspaper, a magazine, or even a newsletter, podcast, or blog. Your audience for a press release is always the person who influences other people.

In the past, press releases would arrive to an editor's desk and they would review them, one by one, usually giving three to five SECONDS per release.

To increase your chances, make sure you know the interests of the editor. Don't just put your content on the Internet and hope someone sees it. After all, you wrote the release because you think it has important news. Send it to the editor who you think will agree with you.

Be careful here. The biggest error is to be caught up with the importance of your own press release, your own product, or your own service. To be successful you absolutely must approach the press release from the position of the editor.

Ask yourself this:

How does my press release help this editor tell a story to their readers?

Can it be a feature list of the product or a list of the problems you think it your product solves? No. It has to be a problem or issue that the editor thinks is important, something that they value.

Do your homework, know your audience, and know the target message.

Here is an example.

One time, I went to work for a large public company, and I had already dealt with the press and media for a few years, having been on CNN and ABC, as well as having been quoted in a number of publications from Wired, to Computerworld, to Maxim. Nevertheless, it was mandatory that each new employee go through media training before they could talk to the press. I showed up for my training with another employee who I'll call "Melvin."

Melvin was a cocky, arrogant, tech-savvy person, who knew his product inside and out. He wasn't even sure why he was at the training. He didn't see how this class was going to teach him anything he didn't already know. The instructor was the principal at an outside PR agency who had been brought in to teach us PR basics.

Me? I didn't mention that I had any previous experience or that I didn't feel it was necessary. I figured that if they thought I needed to get training to talk to the press, it was fine with me.

The instructor, I'll call her "Brenda," went through the basics of speaking with the press, how to stay on topic, and how to focus on problems and issues rather than features and products. It wasn't a bad class. Except for the audible exasperating sounds coming from Melvin, the class was rather enjoyable.

Brenda asked each of us to pretend that we were meeting with a publication of our choosing. We were going to role-play and we would make a pitch about the upcoming release of our product.

You guessed it...Melvin went first. For the entire time, he went on and on about the latest features in product version x.2.3, how it had been changed and upgraded. Not once did he mention his customers, nor the issues they dealt with in their business that this product was supposed to solve. It was all techno babble. Though I wasn't surprised, I admit, I was appalled.

And then it was my turn. I announced that I was visiting Fortune magazine. The instructor's eyebrows lifted in surprise.

I explained that Fortune magazine targets readers who are interested in trends in business. Moreover, since my products were part of an emerging trend, namely mobility, then a Fortune editor would be interested in a story about a trend affecting his or her readers.

My pitch focused almost exclusively on the issues facing business as they began to grapple with employees and data in a mobile environment. Only near the end, did I address how my product/solution, address these emerging challenges.

Brenda was very surprised, she immediately knew that I had done this before, and was impressed with the message.

On the other hand, Melvin was irritated and outright hostile. He began, in an elevated voice, to criticize my approach saying that I had never talked about the features of my product, nor its capabilities, nor even really mentioned my company at all. I obviously didn't understand that it was more important to talk about the product than the problem.

Trust me when I say that you will regularly run into the Melvins of the world (I apologize to anyone named Melvin, I had to make up a name and yours came up).

Just remember, if you know your audience, if you know your message, you can bypass the Melvins and find success with your next pitch to the press.

BlissPoint #7: Inclusive but Exclusive

Kids like to belong to groups and when you are the new kid in class, you are definitely on the outside, looking in. But in almost every school, and nearly every time I started new, a kid would come up to me and introduce himself. As an adult looking back I can now see that these kids, every time, were part of the non-inclusive group. They were on the outside, just like me. To this day I still hold found memories for their acts of kindness to reach out to me. They were looking to be part of something and when there were two of us we formed our own group. Thanks to Judy J. in Fairbanks Alaska from the 3rd grade, Danny in Spokane Washington from the 4th grade, Sheila B. in Wells, Minnesota from the 5th grade, and Paul F. in Tekoa Washington from the 6th grade. I only knew them for a few months but they each left their mark and made a memory that has helped shape into who I am today. I thank them for including me.

You are either in one group or out of one, feeling included or excluded. It seems to be a normal rite of passage as a young person.

As you may remember, my case was more different than most. I attended fourteen schools in seven years, with my family moving every year, often multiple times during the year. I was always the new kid, always the kid who wasn't part of the group, always on the outside looking in.

All of that moving, changing, and attempting to fit in, gave me a very personal appreciation for what it feels like to be the person on the outside, the person who is feeling alone.

That feeling is what helps to shape many of my personal philosophies as a marketing person.

It was during one of my speaking engagements, as I stood in front of a room of hundreds of people, that it hit me: I knew why these people were here. Many of them wanted to know that they were not alone in their business opinions, views, and decisions. I also realized that it could be quite possible that they were feeling alone even though they were surrounded by a room of hundreds of others.

As a public speaker, a conference coordinator, or the Master of Ceremonies at your high school reunion, you have a responsibility to reach out to your audience and bring them together, to find the common thing that everyone in the room, the auditorium, or the stadium is sharing and feeling.

In my case, I took that responsibility and helped everyone feel like they were members of an exclusive club, and I did it with four simple words.

I Am Not Alone

These simple words carry a tremendous amount of power. Each of us feels alone at some point, whether it is in our personal lives or while we're at work, we sometimes wonder if anyone really understands or appreciates how we feel.

As I travel the world speaking and teaching, I'm struck by how much we share in common, whether it is the personal or the professional challenges we face. Isolation or geographical distance can make it seem as though we are the only ones with a specific challenge—that we are only ones who feel alone.

It just isn't true. We are surrounded by other people who are feeling and experiencing the exact same things we are. But people are hesitant to open up about these kinds of feelings, especially in a public or business setting, where social norms and expectations of behavior inhibit our impulse to share.

During the speaking engagement, while I was standing in front of those people, that I could see it in their faces: they felt alone. I told them that they were probably feeling that they were alone and had come to this conference because they wanted to learn how to solve the challenges they faced, that they felt they were the only ones on the planet with their unique issues.

I watched as the majority of audience members smiled and nodded, giving me the confirmation that I was speaking directly to them.

"I want you to repeat after me," I said. "I want you to look around you, see all these people, and I want you to repeat these four words..."

"I am not alone."

The first reaction—it's always is the same—is nervous laughter. The audience members were probably thinking, "Is he really going to make us do this?"

Yes I was.

Then, with everyone watching, I began a countdown: "3, 2, 1...I Am Not Alone."

There was a general mumble and murmur as people made noise with their mouths but did not want to stand out from the crowd. I didn't give up.

"That was not good enough. Let's do this again. I Am Not Alone."

The second time around, the smiles were bigger, the laughter was genuine, and people were getting into it. The volume had risen significantly. You can't stop at this point. You have to drive it home.

"We can do better than that. One more time! I AM NOT ALONE!"

On the third time, the entire room...hundreds of people...were practically shouting out those four words. The mind is an interesting thing. Whatever we tell it, it will believe, and by having a person shout out these words, in a crowded room, it caused them to believe.

But there is one more thing I had to do to really break down the barriers and make the room come together.

"I now want you to turn to the person next to you and say, 'You Are Not Alone'."

Now the room breaks into laughter, talking, smiles, and genuine camaraderie as the barriers come down even further. I could sense that the people felt that they belonged to each other, and belonged to something outside themselves. They were in a safe environment surrounded by friends.

Helping people feel they belong to something and that you understand their pain, their concern, or their situation is a powerful way to stand out. This process can help to make your event, conference, or class become something more than a simple lecture.

Creating the Ecosystem

As part of the process of helping people feel like they belong, extend this to include the company itself. Oftentimes, when doing business, you find yourself surrounded by people and companies who are just trying to figure it out. We are all on different waypoints in our journey through life, and we can all learn from each other.

Having taken this belief to heart, I have always felt that it was important to try to help build up those around me, as a part of my plan for success.

I have found myself at both ends of the spectrum as a vendor. I have been the big player, carrying the well-known brand, and I have been the little guy, just starting out attempting to find a way to make it work. In both cases, I have discovered, that by working with others, and by bringing other companies together, it often helps me, them, and helps our joint customers.

It is the process of creating an ecosystem.

People seldom like to take chances. A buying decision is often made with influence from the community that the person identifies with. This is true for car shopping, clothes shopping, or shopping for products and services as well as shopping as a business. You want to have a sense of individuality, but not too much of it.

As a vendor, realize that your product or service has an impact on other products and services that don't necessarily compete with you, but they still influence the decision.

Understanding this, I have always attempted to create an ecosystem that meets the needs of the customers.

As a smaller player, I found ways to help the bigger vendor. People see a big vendor as a single entity, almost as a person, when in reality each organization is made up of groups of people inside the organization.

Each of those groups has their own challenges, and can even be at odds with other parts of the same company.

Here's what this means: a smaller vendor, who is more nimble and more focused, can provide benefits to a bigger vendor because the bigger vendor cannot bring to bear all their resources in a timely manner.

For example, my company had a product that was heavily reliant on another vendor's product. That product was extremely important to me, but marginally important to the much bigger company. I would occasionally get their attention, but it was often too little too late, since the bigger company dealt with other issues and couldn't give me 100% of their effort or focus.

I created a series of city to city tours around the world that focused on my partner's products rather than mine. I was able to host these city tours for 60% less money than my bigger partner. I simply had the time and focus to get it done.

I then turned around and approached the smaller vendors in my space—companies who simply did not have the resources to host or execute on a massive tour, but who could provide limited things like brochures or other materials, allowing them to be visible during the event, without the large capital outlay.

By doing this, the likelihood of having a customer attend increased dramatically. Topics covered included messaging security, mobility, disaster recovery, spam, and a wide range of other topics. Even though I was organizing and executing on the event, and even though my content made up about 20% of the total, everyone benefited by creating a sense of community with everyone sharing the success rather than attempting to go it alone.

This created another benefit as well. It protected the ecosystem from poisonous behavior by other vendors. Here's what I mean by that. Another big vendor had begun a similar process, working with the other small vendors, by forming partnerships, and selling services to the customer base.   Unfortunately, in time, each partnership ended badly because of broken contracts, broken promises, and bad feelings. It got so bad that lawyers became involved, when the smaller vendors attempted to protect themselves from this big vendor that was acting unethically.

When something like this happens, everyone loses. Customers don't care about the details, they just know that if they make a purchase, there is a chance that there will be drama of some sort. Their purchase could come back to embarrass them or even threaten their job.

Building a healthy ecosystem is essential to mitigating the damage that a single vendor can create when they aren't playing nicely in the sand box.

BlissPoint #8: Building your Fan Base

Our friends are often our biggest fans. They know us, both the good and the bad, and yet still continue to believe in us. It often takes time to build up friendships. Shared experiences, shared lives, all these things need to be present to create that bond. But when you move every year and have to build new relationships every time, the continuity is lost. It wasn't until I was a teenager and we had stopped moving around that I began to form long lasting bonds of friendship. And now as an adult, I know how hard it is in life to have the time to cultivate strong relationships. I'm a big fan of my two brothers who shared most of my childhood journey. Take care of your friends and your fans because you won't get another chance.

Finish this line:

"People do business with people they ..."

Although there is no wrong answer to this, there is a common one. Oftentimes people will say the word "Trust," but I think that there is a better word to finish this sentence.

"People do business with people they LIKE."

There have been many times when I made a purchase, not on impulse, but on "Likepulse." I made the purchase simply because I liked the person. Other times, I've really, really, *really* wanted to buy something, but the person making the sale just didn't make me feel right. I didn't want to buy from them, even though I wanted to buy.

Let me give you an example:

I own timeshare that I really enjoy. I use it regularly and I always have a good time when I visit. One year, my wife and I planned to spend our anniversary in Hawaii. We were married on Valentine's Day and were headed to the island to celebrate. This trip was going to be our present to each other. As a bonus, we got tickets to the NFL Pro Bowl which was happening at the same time (The tickets were her idea. She's a bigger football fan than I am).

Three days before our trip, I called the property in Hawaii to make sure that everything was set and ready to go—something I always do because of frequent traveling.

Unfortunately, the property had no record of our reservation. After further investigation, it was explained that we had canceled the reservation approximately two months earlier. This was quite incorrect. We had not canceled anything. Somehow, a mistake had been made when I had placed a call two months earlier to look at upgrading to a bigger unit. Nothing about our plans had changed. The call was simply to inquire about the possibility of an upgrade, but somehow, the operator took my inquiry as a cancellation of the reservation.

The even bigger challenge that I faced was dealing with two different organizations. My timeshare property uses a third-party vendor who handles transfers. I had transferred my timeshare to a week in Hawaii. Both companies were saying, sorry and there was nothing they could do, I had canceled...it was sold out, and I was out of luck. I was furious. There went our anniversary week. You should have seen the look of amazement and disappointment on my wife's face. How do you think that made me feel? One misunderstanding and there went all of our plans!

For the entire year, each time I had to call either company, I still let them know how unhappy I was, and each time, all I got was the "We're really sorry but there isn't anything we can do."

Building Fans: Keep in Touch to Keep Your Fans

Two years later, I was planning another trip to Hawaii, but this time, it was for two weeks before Thanksgiving and we were bringing friends and family.

I got on the phone, and yet one more time, told my story. I was still angry, mainly because a company that I had enjoyed working with, that I really liked, had left such a bitter taste in my mouth that I didn't believe I could ever enjoy working with them, much less recommending them again.

As I spoke on the call, making the arrangements, I had to have two people on the call, one from each company to handle the transfer of my property for the additional week. I wanted to make sure that nobody could misunderstand my request and that both companies could accommodate my needs and plans.

I then mentioned how upset I had been 18 months earlier when all my travel plans had been killed by the two companies that these two individuals worked for. Yes...I know that it isn't fair to continue to vent at someone who didn't have anything to do with it, but I had not achieved any sense of closure. My customer service needs had not been met.

These gentlemen listened to my story, both expressed their regret, and then I got a surprise: both of them said that they would try to see what they could do to make things right.

They spoke with each other on the conference call, discussing ideas, deals, and made suggestions to each other. They did not know each other, had never met, and worked hundreds of miles apart, but they acted like a focused team to address my grievance.

After a while, they came back to me and said that they could take care of my two weeks, and that in addition to being able to reserve my two weeks for Thanksgiving, they were also willing to upgrade one of my weeks to a three-bedroom suite that slept 12 people. They wanted to know if this would be alright with me. I was thrilled!

A three-bedroom timeshare at a top resort in Hawaii was a dream comes true! This option meant that I would not need to get extra rooms to accommodate all the friends and family. It was a perfect solution and I was humbled by their efforts.

These two gentlemen had gone the extra mile to take my problem and pain, and find a way to resolve it, even though they had nothing to do with causing it. They simply wanted to make sure I was taken care of.

Needless to say, my attitude toward both companies changed. I now confidently share with friends, with family, and with you, about my satisfaction with my timeshare and the wonderful experiences I have had. Did I have a bad experience once? Yes, I did, but that is okay, my two new friends took care of me.

BlissPoint #9: Stealing the Show

When I was 10, I participated in my only Science Fair. The comet Kohoutek had appeared that year and it had been billed as the "Comet of the Century." Unfortunately it didn't live up to its hype. My Science Fair project was about Comet Kohoutek and comets in general. I worked on the stand-up display, created a comet out of a delicately crafted, yet wadded-up piece of paper with a long paper tail. I researched all kinds of facts about comets, wrote them down and glued them to my poster board display.

The night of the Science Fair came and I was excited! I set up my display with all the other kids and stood around answering questions from adults and judges about the cool aspects of comets. At the end of the evening I won a green ribbon. Before you think that was a good thing, EVERYONE got a green ribbon...just for showing up! The red and blue ribbons were for the smart kids...the ones who had displays with flashing lights, or had built whizzy things that skittered across the table, or had molded the paper mache and chicken wire mountains that spewed lava made from vinegar and baking soda.

I'm not going to say that I was scarred by the experience. But I will say that the participation prize definitely left me with a bad taste in my mouth. That night, I swore that if I was ever going to go to another event like that, I was not going to accept the green ribbon. I was going to stand out! I was going to steal the show.

A company is often faced with a conflict of opportunities when it comes to conferences and tradeshows: there are far more shows to sponsor than there are marketing dollars.

The question asked is this:

How do you determine what the better event is? Is it...

- a small presence at a very large show of more than 30,000 attendees
- a relatively bigger presence at a smaller show
- an event with less than 300 attendees

There are many levels in between, but the point to address is the best event on which to spend your money.

The answer is dependent on your goal. What are you attempting to accomplish by attending the show? I can remember attending a show, Comdex, in the 1990s.

What a waste of time, money, and personnel!

My plan was to get leads, and with 125,000 people in attendance, only a small fraction of those people came to my booth and became active leads. Participation.

In contrast, I attended a legal industry tradeshow in Arizona with 275 attendees. I left the show with 240 business cards and some strong leads. Nearly every person at the show came by my booth and spoke with me. Profit!

The biggest challenge for any marketing person or department is to discover a way to be heard above the noise. Renting out Hummer and giving free rides to a targeted audience is one way to do it, but an easier way is to participate in events where the "noise to attendee" ratio is much more favorable.

Oftentimes you can find a smaller event with a more focused message that allows you to spend significantly less money, yet gain exposure to a much higher percentage of attendees.

The DIY Tradeshow

If you aren't finding the return on investment for the shows you are attending, there is always the option of doing it yourself. Putting on a conference or tradeshow is fairly straight-forward. You find a location...a local hotel is usually the best choice, you arrange for catering, arrange for a single speaker or multiple speakers, and then you sit back and wait for the people to show up.

Except they aren't going to show up if they don't know about it, nor will they show up if the timing is off, the travel is too far, the cost is too high or the content isn't of interest.

Putting on a show is the easy part, making it relevant so that someone attends is the hard part.

It is All About Perception

I found myself in the conference business quite by accident. My market had a fairly big central conference that was held every year and thousands of people attended. Nearly 100% of my customers knew of the conference, and many had attended at one time or the other over the 20 years that the event had been hosted.

Then one day, a small conference company created a similar event, but on a vastly smaller scale. A few hundred people planned on being in attendance vs. the thousands for the bigger event.

The small conference company had a formula that they used when entering into each market, and they applied the formula when they entered into mine.

This time, the cracks in their process appeared. The conference company didn't want to adjust to specific needs of the market they had entered, and they certainly didn't like to include vendors of any kind. This event was not a vehicle for vendors to sell products. To their minds, vendors meant product pitching, and this company's conference was focused on the needs of the end user.

I was one of those vendors! We tried to offer to help mold the conference into something that would benefit all vendors, as well as being beneficial to the attendees, but we got nowhere with this company.

That's when I decided I needed to hold my own conference. But there were many things that had to be considered:

- Timing
- Location
- Cost
- Content

Timing was important. The big conference, BrainShare, was in March in Salt Lake City. The smaller conference, Advisor, was being held in Aug/Sept in Phoenix. This meant we needed to pick a time that would not conflict with these two events. We chose January.

January had several advantages. It was at the very beginning of the calendar year, which meant that we got the first shot at travel budgets for prospective clients. Second, after a solid month of holidays in the US, including Thanksgiving in late November, Christmas and Hanukkah in December, and New Year's Day on the first of January, people were ready to get back to work. The only holiday in January to contend with was Martin Luther King Jr. Day, so the event was scheduled for the weekend after this holiday.

That brings up the other item: the when. At which time of the week would we hold our event? In the United States, people have certain tendencies around the days of the week. Monday and Friday are believed to be low productivity days. We made the unusual decision to start our event on Sunday and go until Tuesday.

Originally it was going to be a Monday and Tuesday only event, but our event blossomed. On Sunday night, when people arrived we created an evening dinner. By the second year, so many people were arriving on Sunday, that we turned it into a full training day. Then, people began arriving on Saturday, which we turned into the bonus day. Suddenly our small, two day conference, was now running Saturday through Tuesday.

Now, the thing is the comments that I've received about holding an event on a weekend. Our attendees loved it! Our event allowed them to come and spend two days in training during non-work days, then spend all day Monday at the event, fly home the evening of Tuesday, then arrive back at work on Wednesday. They'd finished a four-day conference and still had more than half of the work week available.

This became a very important part of the event. Our attendees are hard working people. Sometimes, it can be difficult to convince your boss that you need time off to go get training to do your job better. It becomes much easier when you can explain to your boss that you will be taking two of your own personal days to attend, only costing the company two work days for a four day conference.

This small decision on our part created an ongoing incentive for employers to send their employees to our conferences because they were getting much more for their money.

Location

If you are going to hold a nationwide conference in January there are a few restrictions on location. We had to come up with a location that would work for the majority of customers, was easy to travel to, had the facilities we needed, and above all else was accessible in January.

Our choice came down to the Dallas/Ft. Worth area for several reasons. First, since Southwest Airlines had a hub there, it meant that most of our attendees could travel to the region inexpensively.

Dallas would normally mean mild weather in January, which would minimize potential traffic delays and make overall logistics easier.

An added bonus was that Texas had a large number of customers who would be able to travel without leaving the state—something that is important when considering budgets.

The other location to consider was the facility itself. Not all conference facilities are the same. In our case we needed a hotel with a fairly low price point but with services to meet our needs. We also needed other hotels within walking distance for overflow.

When working with hotels there are two things the hotel wants to know.

- How much catering will be necessary?
- How many hotel room nights are required?

These two items become negotiable and form the full basis of your costs. Seldom do you actually rent or pay for the conference space itself unless you are only working with a conference center.

The hotel makes all their money on room nights and food catering and is almost always willing to give up any kind of conference room fees.

Cost

Depending on your objectives and goals for the event, the conference doesn't have to be expensive, either. But remember, your attendees will judge your company, your products, and your services by the quality and emotional impact of the event.

Simply put, that means this: don't be cheap and don't skimp on the little stuff simply to save a dollar. It will do more damage to your brand and business than simply paying for it.

In my case I was originally creating a conference to allow my customers and potential customers a place to come for training on our latest products.

We didn't even have to break even from a cost standpoint. Because this was all about selling the product, I was able to spend money that was later recouped through increased sales.

Then there are the cultural differences to consider. In Europe, the hotel wanted to charge us 3000 Euro for coffee. That is about $4,500 USD. To an American company that is absolutely insane. They were, however, willing to give us all the soda we wanted for free. In the US, the coffee was nearly free, while the sodas were $5 each. Everything is negotiable.

Other items to consider when looking at costs are Audio Visual. Do you want to rent those projectors or simply buy them? Buying them means you get to use them next time, and over and over again. Renting means you usually pay the same amount as buying them, every...single...time.

Your biggest costs by far will be the food: breakfast breaks, lunch breaks, coffee breaks, dinner, and maybe even a cocktail party. The food adds up quickly. I developed a rule of thumb for handling the food budget, a rule that works no matter whether I was in Dallas, Sydney, or Berlin.

To determine total food costs when you are providing meals, plan on approximately 100 units of cost per person per day. This means 100 Euro in Berlin, 100 Australian in Sydney, and 100 US dollars if you are in the United States.

Thus, 100 people for a three day conference are going to cost you:

100 x 3 x 100 = $30,000 in food.

Again, this is if you are providing all three meals and receptions. Food costs are a tricky thing. The hotel will want to know how many people you are planning for each meal. They will then order the food according to the numbers you submitted.

Just because you have 300 people registered for a conference doesn't mean you are going to get 300 people to show up every day for every meal. We learned this the hard way the first time we did a European event.

My European team was doing the food ordering for the first time and simply told the hotel that since 300 people had registered, there would be 300 people at each meal each day.

The hotel ordered the food and then was dismayed, as was our accounting department, when only 100 people showed up for breakfast on day one.

The food bill ended up costing an excess of $30,000 dollars. Know your audience and then focus on their behaviors.

Recovering Costs

There are a few ways to recover your costs and to help offset the high expense of your event. Again, if you are not in the conference business and simply need to break even or operate at a slight loss, there are some pretty straightforward things you can do.

Sponsorship Money

If you are holding a conference for 300 of your closest customers, there is a very good chance that other vendors would also like to be in front of your customers. If you handle it carefully you can create an arrangement that is beneficial for everyone.

Approach other vendors that augment or compliment the needs of your customers. Find the other products that your customers may be interested in. An interesting result of this idea is that your customers will come to see you as a single point of contact for issues that you may not address at all, but the ecosystem of solutions and vendors that you've created will cause them to form an opinion of leadership around your product.

Now don't get greedy with the sponsorship dollars. Remember that you are building a long term branding and marketing vehicle with your conference. Attempting to extract full monetary value on the first event will often poison the opportunity down the road. A little investment on your part will help build the long term success.

With the first few conferences that I held, I attempted to get about 10 vendors, and then to have them contribute about 50% of the estimated costs. If the event was going to cost $100,000, then I was attempting to raise $25,000-$50,000 in sponsorship fees, averaging $2,500-$5,000 per vendor.

This was a very good deal for the vendors. It meant that for 2.5%-5% of the full cost of an event, they were able to get in front of a targeted audience. Additionally, for their co-sponsorship, a vendor always got a chance to present a session. This was extremely important. In order for my conference to be a success I needed to make sure that my attendees came and learned as much as possible.

Oftentimes this meant that they were learning more about other companies than about my own. What I discovered was that there was an emotional satisfaction that came from the attendee's having seen so many solutions presented, that they were more likely to purchase my products and services.

There is an unspoken rule of reciprocal services between companies and customers. If they get a sense that you genuinely care about their needs, they will return that with brand and company loyalty. Remember my timeshare situation? You can't fake it, you have to show them and prove to them that you care. This often means setting their needs before your own. But the return on investment is long term. It's priceless.

When it comes to conferences, this sense of care can be demonstrated by the type of facility, the quality and quantity of the food, the amount of snacks like oatmeal or granola bars during the day...all these items add up to form an overall impression about how much you care about the customer.

They see it, they take notice, and then they return the favor.

Not to point fingers, but this is something that uninformed accounting people struggle with. They only see the spreadsheet costs and focus on the money spent on seemingly frivolous items, and then short change the customer. The customer notices. Don't ever let the accounting people get involved with the planning stages.

Will Speak for Food

There are other costs that you might need to look at that aren't part of the normal budget. This includes the speakers themselves. Believe it or not, but most performers will speak for food. At my event, we would usually find local talent who would be able to come and do a session for the price of a free meal.

Now, sometimes there was that special person that I wanted to have speak, and they really wanted to come my event, but they couldn't afford to pay for the travel and hotel themselves.

The accounting people often told me that I wasn't allowed to pay for speakers to come. We aren't talking about speaking fees, but are simply talking about the cost of travel and lodging. This was the simple craziness that I had to find a way around. Good content comes from good speakers, and if you want people to show up to your conference, make sure you are giving them what they want to hear, not necessarily what you want to tell them.

So to get around this accounting edict, I approached the various sponsors and asked if any of them would be willing to spend a little more money and officially sponsor a speaker. They would pay for the travel and the lodging and then would receive recognition on the website, in the session, and other acknowledgement for their contribution. This way I wasn't paying for the speaker, but instead was getting others to help out.

Another crazy decision I had to overcome was an ongoing one. It takes lots of bodies to run a successful show. You need people to staff the registration, those who handle logistics, you need the gophers, and you need the folks who do all the little things that are often needed. We came up with the solution of flying in volunteers. These were friends and family that were willing to sacrifice time if I paid for airfare, hotel and food.

This worked out well for everyone, and I was especially grateful for the volunteers, until the accountants decided that we weren't going to pay for family members to travel to our events. Instead we would hire the staff from the hotel, at *3 times* the cost. Because the money showed up in a different category, it was approved. Again, sometimes you just have to work with the crazies.

A special mention should go to my brother, Rodney Bliss. He is a certified American Sign Language Interpreter. It isn't his day job, but a need arose at one of our conferences for ASL services.

The cost to go through an agency was wildly prohibitive for what we needed. My brother stepped up and volunteered to help.

He spent nearly the entire four days signing for an attendee who was extremely appreciative to have the service available. My brother signed for 6 to 8 hours a day. If you have ever worked extensively with your hands, imagine attempting to type, non-stop, for 6 hours. At the end of the conference his hands were sore with stiff and swollen fingers and joints. It was a wonderful gesture on his part and one of which I and others will always be appreciative.

Worth the Price of Admission

This is the other way you pay for your conference: get the attendees to pay for the service you are providing. When you are starting a new conference that no one has ever heard of before, it can be a real challenge to get people to pay an entrance fee on top of the other costs of travel and lodging. It can be a showstopper of a challenge.

After a successful event in Dallas we decided to hold an additional event in Sydney, Australia. Our expectations were not set high for success of the event. We were looking for around 100 people to attend—a number that we felt was a modest goal. We promoted the event, pitched the event, talked about the event, and did everything we could to tell *everyone* about the event. The event was to be held the 7-10 of June. By May 21, roughly two weeks before, we had only 13 people registered.

It was going to be a disaster! I had two options:

Option 1: Cancel the show. Even though the public relations fallout would hurt, it would save us the embarrassment of hosting a major event and only having 13 people show up. We had sponsors traveling, we had speakers, and we had all amounts of investments. I felt that with 2 ½ weeks to go, I could do enough damage control to escape with the costs kept to a minimum. This was not my first choice, but it had to be considered.

Option 2: Get creative. The idea was to make the event free of charge. Now, at first this may sound like a no-brainer. What could possibly be bad about offering the conference for free?

Perception, Perception, Perception
Imagine that you are looking to attend to a conference that cost a large amount of money. You really want to go but your boss says it isn't in the budget. You see advertising, you see promotions, and you see all of the attention focused on the event. Then, two weeks before hand, the event announces that they are giving away all the tickets. You get to attend for free?

"Hooray!" you say, and you rush back to your boss and let her know the good news. Except it isn't necessarily good news. Your boss enquires: "Why, are they giving it away for free?" Your boss is smart. She's thinking that no one signed up...that the event wasn't interesting enough to generate enough attendance and now the conference is desperate and trying to give away tickets.

Your boss is right. By giving something away like this for free, it creates a negative impression on the company hosting the event, if the message isn't delivered properly.

I wanted to give the event away for free, if only to boost the numbers up to around 50, if we were lucky. The costs were already sunk. It wasn't going to cost us anything more because we had already committed to numbers. We paid those amounts whether or not anyone showed.

To give it away I had to have a good cover story that would work well with the bosses. That same day, Vodaphone approached us about being a small sponsor of the show. Vodaphone is a very large mobile carrier in Australia, so I went to them and made them a deal. They could be a minor sponsor, but they had to allow me to announce that their sponsorship was making it possible for everyone to attend the show for free. This way Vodaphone got some good exposure, the conference got a boost of confidence, and my attendees, who I knew really wanted to attend, now had a good opportunity to come. Vodaphone agreed and I put out the press release. Within the next two weeks, more than 100 people had registered!

And that's not the end of the story! Within six weeks of the end of the show, my company's sales revenue in Australia jumped 45%. People came, they saw, they bought, and then they told their friends who did the same.

The success of the event had a cascading effect. In the end, the revenue from increased sales justified the cost event, even when we had to give the attendance fees away for free.

Content, Content, Content

Content is king! Without good content, your show, conference, or presentation will fall flat on its face. You may be able to convince people to come the first time, but without good content they won't be coming back. To help ensure that your content is done well, you have to put yourself in the shoes of your prospective attendees.

- What would interest them?
- What is a hot topic right now?

Sometimes these answers aren't necessarily about your product or company. Other times, the content is more about one of your partners, vendors, or sponsors. Don't be turned off by this. When you make a purchase decision, it can be an emotional experience, even when it is business to business. Even if that decision isn't to buy your product immediately, it sets up an emotional relationship with that customer or prospective client. They now feel a sense of obligation or loyalty. That loyalty might not manifest itself immediately, but over time, I promise, you will benefit from the effort.

This was a battle I often fought with inexperienced sales people. They wanted to continually talk about their products and their solutions 100% of the time. To go down this path is to demonstrate to the attendee that you aren't interested in their needs, but instead on simply attempting to sell them something. Remember Melvin?

Some of the biggest compliments I received were from attendees who thanked me for inviting specific vendors, because with their busy job they just wouldn't have had the time to do the research on their own. By being able to come to one place and have it all centralized, I had saved them a lot of time.

Subject Matter Expert

Another secret to being successful with show or presentation content is to become a Subject Matter Expert. This title has several meanings, but in the context of this idea, I'm talking about becoming knowledgeable in a subject that is important to your customer or prospect.

Oftentimes a SME isn't someone who is smarter than us, it is simply someone who has had more time to learn about a topic.

This means, that with a focused application of time, you can become an SME and a resource to your attendees, your prospects, and to your customers.

To be most effective as an SME, you have to learn about the pros and cons of the issue. Sometimes this means understanding when a competitor's product may be better suited, and having the courage to tell the prospect the truth.

This is very important if you want to stand out and build a following. People will trust you more when you tell them the truth that helps them make the right buying decision. It is that trust which establishes relationships that last over time, allowing us to continue to help our customers over time, rather than the pressure of attempting to make a single sale.

Now don't get me wrong on this. Don't give a prospect reasons not to buy your product if they want it, but do be sure to identify whether your product will solve their specific need, and if not, give guidance on the options and solutions to help solve their problem. This takes a tremendous amount of faith.

A salesperson under pressure to make their monthly quota is not going to be inclined to pass up a sale unless they have the discipline to see how they can have more success in the future.

This style of marketing does an interesting thing in the mind of the prospect. Remember, people like to buy things from people they like. If you take care of them, help them, and keep them from making a mistake, loyal customers will find a way to pay you back.

They may not need that feature or service as badly, but they will find reasons to do business with you.

Many people have said it, in many different ways: courage is not the absence of fear, but is the ability to act in spite of your fear.

I love to present, to stand in front of audiences of single individuals, groups of hundreds, or crowds of thousands. But every time before I go on stage, every time before I open my mouth and begin to speak, for the briefest moment, I'm afraid. Fear grips my insides and twists it in knots.

The night before I was about to conduct an eight-hour training session with a group of 200 people, I had a dream that during the training, I informed everyone of their first break. Everyone in the room got up, left, and nobody came back. I woke up mortified.

The next day, I had presented my opening material, and I paused as we came to the first 10-minute break. As the attendees departed, a man approached me. He said that he wanted to apologize because he had to leave. His reason? He discovered that he was in the wrong session, and had realized this shortly after I began speaking and presenting, but he was enjoying my presentation so much, that he decided to sit through the first hour even though he had no idea what I was talking about. My fears subsided.

So, no matter what it is that you do, whether it's participating in an event, putting together a presentation, developing your press release, or passing out that spiffy giveaway, I hope that you can find ways to creatively consider your audience. Look for the value and overcome the fears that keep you from stepping out on stage, whatever that stage may be. I look forward to hearing how you found your own ways to do so—to not accept the green ribbon of participation, but to act in courage, with confidence.

Go ahead! Steal the show.

www.ingramcontent.com/pod-product-compliance
Lightning Source LLC
Chambersburg PA
CBHW022129170526
45157CB00004B/1801